The Brigh
9.3 miles (
Studio just west of Bright Angel Lodge to Bright
Angel Campground at the bottom of the canyon near
Phantom Ranch. The first 4.6 miles (7.4 km) of the
trail descend along the Bright Angel Fault to Indian
Garden. There are three resthouses in this section
of the trail. The Mile-and-a-Half and Three-Mile
Resthouses have water most of the time during the
summer months (check maps for locations). Indian
Garden Resthouse has water year-round. Occasional
pipeline breaks shut off the water at the resthouses,
so, before departure, check on the bulletin board at
the trailhead or ask at the Backcountry Information
Center by Maswik Lodge for current water availability
along the trail. Upon leaving Indian Garden, the trail
follows Pipe and Garden Creeks for 3.1 miles (5 km)
to the Colorado River. The next 1.6 miles (2.6 km)
follow the Colorado River upstream via the River Trail.
The descent from rim to river takes approximately
four to five hours; plan eight to nine hours for the
ascent. *Do not attempt to hike from the rim to the
river and back in one day.*

DAY HIKES

There are several possibilities for day hikes along the Bright Angel Trail. Water requirements range from ½ quart (½ liter) to 1 quart (1 liter) for every hour spent hiking. It is also important to eat well and snack often. During the summer months it is best to hike before 10:00 AM or after 4:00 PM, avoiding the hottest part of the day. Remember that it will probably take you twice as long to hike out as it did to hike in. The ease of walking downhill often lures hikers to proceed farther than they should. To help prevent emergencies, volunteer park rangers patrol the Bright Angel and other corridor trails, providing advice and assistance.

Popular day hikes along the Bright Angel Trail include:

D Mile-and-a-Half Resthouse
3 miles (4.8 km) round-trip distance
2.5 hours round-trip hiking time

F Three-Mile Resthouse
6 miles (9.7 km) round-trip distance
5 hours round-trip hiking time

H Indian Garden*
9.2 miles (14.8 km) round-trip distance
7 hours round-trip hiking time

Plateau Point*
12.2 miles (19.6 km) round-trip distance
9 hours round-trip hiking time

* *During the summer months, day hikes to Indian Garden and Plateau Point are not recommended due to the heat and the strenuous ascent.*

For hundreds of years humans have traveled along the Bright Angel Trail. There are two reasons that it is one of the earliest and most-used trails from the South Rim: water and accessibility. The springs at Indian Garden produce more potable water than others along the south side of the canyon, and the Bright Angel Fault creates a natural break in the cliffs, making it relatively easy to reach those springs.

Both prehistoric and historic American Indians used the trail and raised crops along Garden Creek. Evidence of this occupation can be seen in the form of pictographs along the trail above Indian Garden.

tographs along Bright Angel Trail

Miners began using the route in the late 1800s. In 1890–91, Pete Berry and brothers Niles and Ralph Cameron widened the trail in the hope of exploiting mineral deposits in the area. It did not take long to realize, however, that the real riches lay in tourism and not in ore. Operating it as a toll road, Ralph Cameron charged $1 for its use. He guaranteed control by filing dubious mining claims at scenic points along the rim, on the trail, and at Indian Garden. Eventually these claims totaled more than 13,000 acres (5,260 ha) and threatened to monopolize the tourist trade at the canyon.

The Santa Fe Railway, which reached the canyon in 1901, filed suit challenging Cameron's claims, and years of litigation ensued. These claims were finally invalidated in 1920, but for years Cameron controlled access into the canyon along the Bright Angel Trail.

The Bright Angel Trail subsequently passed into the hands of Coconino County, which offered it to the National Park Service in 1928 in exchange for an access road to the canyon from Williams, fifty-four miles (87 km) south of the canyon.

In order to reach Phantom Ranch prior to 1936, hikers and mule riders headed east from Indian Garden through Burro Spring following what is today the Tonto Trail. During 1933–36, the Civilian Conservation Corps constructed the River Trail, and the National Park Service improved the lower section of the Bright Angel Trail.

Use of the Bright Angel remains high throughout the year except during the coldest months. What was once a prehistoric trail is now part of a cross-canyon corridor hiked by over one hundred thousand people a year.

GEOLOGY ALONG THE TRAIL

As you stand at the trailhead you may speculate about the origin of this incredible landscape. Three elements came into play in the formation of Grand Canyon.

First, there had to be elevation. You are standing on what was once a much taller, flat, expansive plateau composed of various rock layers.

Second, the forces of erosion had to be brought about by running water, helped by the freeze-thaw cycle, chemical weathering (a process by which exposure to certain elements such as air or water cause a chemical alteration in the mineral content of rock), and wind. A large river like the Colorado, fed by mountain snows and flowing across an arid land, is a master cutter. Minimal rainfall retards soil development and hinders growth of vegetation, which leads to rapid erosion into cliffs and terraces.

The third element is time. Grand Canyon, with the Colorado River following its present course, began forming between five and six million years ago, and it continues to evolve today.

Grand Canyon exposes a history of the earth that is unmatched elsewhere. As you look below, each distinct cliff and terrace represents an era. Each horizontal band of rock tells of the time and circumstances under which it was deposited—long before the cutting of the canyon. The rock strata in this mile-deep chasm carries you back nearly two billion years. Geologists study the rock layers for their structure, chemical composition, and age. Paleontologists study the fossils they find in the rock. They combine this information to determine how the rock was formed, what the environment was like at the time, and what forms of life prevailed.

The Battleship, a canyon butte that resembles a navy vessel, towers over the Bright Angel Trail.

ECOLOGY ALONG THE TRAIL

While the rock strata contain stories of living things in the past, the present Grand Canyon contains a tremendous diversity of life. The Bright Angel Trail passes through several distinct habitats. Each differs in the amount of water, kind and depth of soil, range of temperatures, and elevation. These, in turn, affect the distribution of plant and animal species that will be found in a given habitat.

Climate in Grand Canyon varies greatly between the river and the rim. Differences in elevation play a major role. At the river, 2,400 feet (732 m) above sea level, the temperature is an average of 20 degrees F (6.7 °C) warmer than that on the South Rim, 7,000 feet (2,133 m) above sea level. Exposed rock retains heat and contributes to typically high temperatures. Elevation also affects precipitation. The Inner Gorge is shielded from weather fronts that affect the rim plateaus. Often, rain falling at rim level will evaporate before it reaches the canyon bottom. This explains

Park maintenance staff shoveling snow near the trailhead after a major blizzard, January 27, 1949

why the South Rim receives an average of 16 inches (41 cm) of precipitation per year, while the Inner Gorge receives only 8 inches (20 cm) annually. Plant and animal adaptation to these differences is an interesting part of the canyon's story.

All the habitat types in Grand Canyon and their associated fauna and flora have one thing in common: Every living system is a complex network of shared energy and resources. As in all ecosystems, interdependence and interaction are essential.

THE TRAILHEAD

At the trailhead and along the upper sections of the Bright Angel Trail you are in the pinyon-juniper forest habitat. Thunderstorms in the summer and snow in the winter provide the precipitation necessary to maintain this type of

Ellsworth and Emery Kolb stand outside Kolb Studio next to the trailhead, circa 1904.

vegetation. The shallow and rocky soil is not capable of retaining moisture for long periods of time because the runoff and evaporation rates are high.

The short-needled pinyon pine (*Pinus edulis*) and the predominate scaly-leaved Utah juniper (*Juniperus osteosperma*) have adapted to this environment in a number of ways. Their modest foliage and thick bark limit moisture loss and resist temperature extremes, while their extensive, shallow root systems help them gather water quickly. They also limit water waste by growing slowly—many of the trees around you are over one hundred years old.

A BRIGHT ANGEL TRAILHEAD TO:

Mile-and-a-Half Resthouse
1.5 miles (2.4 km)

Three-Mile Resthouse
3.0 miles (4.8 km)

Indian Garden
4.6 miles (7.4 km)

Plateau Point
6.1 miles (10.0 km)

River Trail Junction
7.7 miles (12.4 km)

Bright Angel Campground
9.3 miles (15.0 km)

Phantom Ranch
9.6 miles (15.4 km)

North Kaibab Trailhead
23.4 miles (37.7 km)

H INDIAN GARDEN TO:

Bright Angel Trailhead
4.6 miles (7.4 km)

Plateau Point
1.5 miles (2.4 km)

River Trail Junction
3.1 miles (5.0 km)

Bright Angel Campground
4.7 miles (7.6 km)

Phantom Ranch
5.0 miles (8.0 km)

The + Battleship

Maricopa Point

Redwall Limestone
Muav Limestone

Trailview Overlook

Jacobs Ladder G

Rim Trail

Two-Mile Corner E

Hermit Supai

Coconino Sandstone
Hermit Formation

Toroweap Formation
Coconino Sandstone

D M

Second Tunnel C

Kaibab Formation
Toroweap Formation

Kolb Studio

Bright Angel Lodge

El Tovar

First Tunnel B A

Grand Canyon Railway

Hermit Road

Trailhead
6,860 ft (2,091 m)

🥾 Backcountry Information Center

0 — 0.5 Kilometer

0 — 0.5 Miles

10

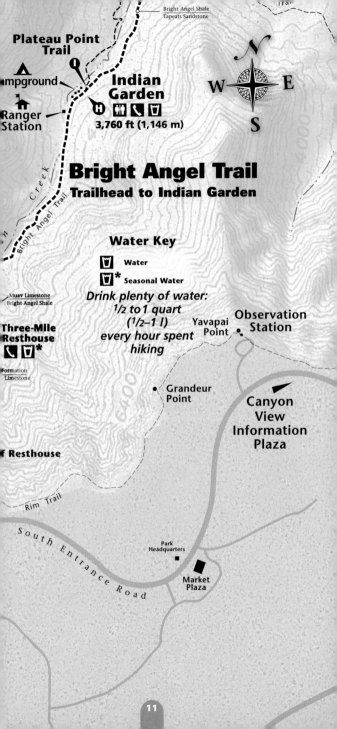

Plateau Point Trail

⛺ Campground

🏠 **Ranger Station**

Bright Angel Shale
Tapeats Sandstone

Indian Garden

🚹🚻 📞 💧
3,760 ft (1,146 m)

Bright Angel Trail
Trailhead to Indian Garden

Water Key

💧 Water

💧* Seasonal Water

*Drink plenty of water:
¹/₂ to 1 quart
(¹/₂–1 l)
every hour spent
hiking*

Muav Limestone
Bright Angel Shale

Three-Mile Resthouse
📞 💧*

Formation
Limestone

Yavapai Point

Observation Station

Canyon View Information Plaza

• Grandeur Point

Resthouse
📞 💧*

Rim Trail

South Entrance Road

Park Headquarters •

Market Plaza

Kolb Studio is perched on the rim of the canyon near the Bright Angel trailhead (the trail can be accessed from Kolb Studio or from a second trailhead a few hundred yards west of the building near the mule corral). Established in 1904 by Ellsworth and Emery Kolb, the studio was in operation until his death in 1976. Emery and Ellsworth took pictures of mule parties descending the Bright Angel Trail and sold them to participants. Because water available to the Kolbs on the rim was not pure enough for processing photographs, the brothers maintained a developing room at Indian Garden until a pipeline was built from there to the rim in 1932. The darkroom at Indian Garden required taking the photographs, hiking to the darkroom, developing and printing the images, and getting back out ahead of the mule parties in order to sell the prints.

Today, the National Park Service owns and the Grand Canyon Association operates a bookstore and exhibit gallery in the historic structure.

Captian John Hance leads the mule party of William Jennings Bryan (last mule rider) down the old Bright Angel Trail. Kolb brothers photo, circa 1904.

Kaibab
Formation

Toroweap
Formation

Coconino
Sandstone

Hermit
Shale

THE FIRST TUNNEL

The top section of the Bright Angel Trail traverses
the Kaibab Formation. Marine fossils of brachiopods
(primitive shellfish), corals, crinoids, and sponges
enable us to determine that 270 million years ago this
area was covered by a warm, shallow sea. Sands and
calcium carbonate (lime) settled as sludge on the sea
floor and hardened into the limestone of the Kaibab
Formation. Chert nodules, composed of silica, can
also be seen in the rock. In many cases, the silica
precipitated out of the sea water and replaced the
minerals in sponges and shelled animals, leading to
their fossilization.

The Toroweap Formation, the next layer below
the Kaibab Formation, reflects the same kind of past
environment. The land was low, the climate warm, and
a varied population of marine organisms similar to those
in the Kaibab Formation flourished in an ancient sea.

To the left and above you after you pass through the First Tunnel lies Mallery's Grotto, a panel of American Indian pictographs. These painted images span many centuries, and the Havasupai Indians, who today live on a reservation in the western Grand Canyon, created some of them. This archeological site can only be viewed from the trail and is protected by law from vandalism, which includes writing or scratching your name or initials on the rock. Even touching will damage the paintings through contact with the skin's natural oils.

THE SECOND TUNNEL

This portion of Grand Canyon has been cut through the surrounding Kaibab Plateau. Uplift enabled the plateau to reach its current elevation. Even though this uplift was gradual, it was accompanied by faulting and cracking of the rock.

At the Second Tunnel, you are standing on the Bright Angel Fault, which crosses the canyon and extends for miles on either side. You can see that the rocks to the west are uplifted 189 feet (58 m) higher than those to the east. Erosion has accelerated along this natural break in the rock layers and formed the side canyon in which you are hiking.

At this point you are at the top of the buff-colored Coconino Sandstone. In contrast to the layers above you, the Coconino Sandstone was deposited about 275 million years ago when much of northern Arizona was covered by an enormous desert. Sand dunes hundreds of feet high were constantly moved by wind, and cross-bedding of the sand resulted. The sea that formed the Toroweap Formation above covered these dunes and deposited muds and more sand on top of them. Minerals seeping into the dunes

and pressure from above formed the Coconino. While no skeletal remains have been found in this layer, the fossilized tracks of several species of reptiles have been identified.

MILE-AND-A-HALF RESTHOUSE

Above the resthouse and below the north-facing cliffs of the Coconino Sandstone, temperatures are cooler because of slightly more shade and moisture. These subtle differences create a microclimate that allows Douglas-fir (*Pseudotsuga menziesii*) to exist. While this species is common on the North Rim, on the south side of the canyon such trees exist primarily under these special conditions, although a few such trees populate the South Rim. Gambel oak (*Quercus gambelii*) is also commonly found around the resthouse.

By the time you reach the resthouse, you have already passed through millions of years of the earth's history. This resthouse, with a composting toilet, seasonal water, and an emergency phone, is in the Hermit Formation. This formation, like the Supai Group below it, is composed of shales (hardened muds) and sandstones deposited in a swampy,

Coconino
Sandstone

Hermit
Shale

Supai
Group

terrestrial environment. Fossils in the Hermit consist of ferns and cone-bearing plants, while in the Supai there are tracks of reptiles and amphibians. In other parts of North America, the great coal-forming swamps abounded when the Hermit formed, and dense vegetation covered the land. The pine and juniper here today are relatives of the plants that began developing at that time.

The Civilian Conservation Corps constructed Mile-and-a-Half, Three-Mile, Indian Garden, and River Resthouses of native stone in 1935-36.

E TWO-MILE CORNER

The rocks in this area are covered with lichens. A combination of a fungus and an algae, lichens colonize niches that other plants cannot. Living on dry, bare rock, lichens grow very slowly, and their regeneration rate is extremely slow—some are more than one thousand years old. The fungal covering of this plant secretes an acid which breaks down the rock on which it lives. Enough soil will eventually be produced so that mosses can establish themselves. Mosses continue the process of breaking down the rock and leaving organic debris until enough soil has formed to support a community of grasses, shrubs, and, eventually, trees.

THREE-MILE RESTHOUSE

The sheer Redwall cliff below Three-Mile Resthouse is the dividing line between forest and desert-scrub habitats. Climatic conditions above are typically hot and dry in the summer, and cold and snowy in the winter. Trees and shrubs in this habitat exhibit characteristics typical of lower-elevation desert flora.

The Bright Angel Trail wriggles up to Three-Mile Resthouse at the top of the Redwall Formation.

Leaf surfaces are small to prevent water loss, and root systems have developed to enable them to gather water quickly when it becomes available. Vegetation is sparse and close to the ground. Here, as in any habitat, there is a compromise between growth and adaptation to the characteristics of the environment.

By this time, you have probably seen the common raven (*Corvus corax*) soaring on thermal drafts created as warm air rises out of the canyon. These large birds, permanent residents of Grand Canyon, are found throughout the western United States. A much larger bird, with a wingspan of up to 9½ feet (2.9 m), also frequents the skies and rocky ledges above the Bright Angel Trail. The California condor (*Gymnogyps californianus*) was last observed in the

Redwall
Limestone

Muav
Limestone

View from just below Three-Mile Resthou

Grand Canyon region in 1924; in 1996 wildlife biologists began a program to reintroduce them to northern Arizona. The biologists' goal is to establish a self-sustaining population.

The Redwall Limestone below the resthouse is one of the most prominent layers in the canyon, in many places reaching a height of five hundred feet (155 m). Composed of almost pure limestone, this layer was deposited about 340 million years ago when this area was covered by a warm sea similar to the Caribbean. Life within this ancient sea teemed with various species of plants and animals. Fish and invertebrates like nautiloids, corals, and brachiopods had already developed.

Limestone is gray or white in color, but running water leaches iron compounds from the Hermit and Supai formations above and gives the Redwall its distinctive color. Limestone is water soluble, which accounts for the numerous caves, alcoves, and amphitheatres that are found in this formation. A path behind the resthouse leads to a viewpoint looking down the Redwall and out to Indian Garden and Plateau Point.

To the east of this trail is a pile of planks and debris—the remains of a tramway built in 1932 to aid in the construction of a water pipeline from Indian Garden to the South Rim.

JACOBS LADDER TO INDIAN GARDEN

As one of the widest bands of continuously exposed rock, the Redwall Limestone makes travel into and out of the canyon difficult. Generally, getting through the Redwall is impossible unless you reach a fault zone that creates a break in this sheer cliff. Jacobs Ladder, the set of switchbacks below Three-Mile Resthouse, makes use of the break created by the Bright Angel Fault.

Below the Redwall Limestone, you enter the first rock layer in a series of formations known collectively as the Tonto Group. The Muav Limestone, deposited some 500 million years ago when seas covered this area, slopes downward to the gray-green hills of the Tonto Platform.

Just above Indian Garden, you hike through a number of basins and intermittent stream beds on the upper Tonto Platform. This habitat supports a different vegetational community than is found on the hotter, drier slopes surrounding it. Common in this area are western redbud (*Cercis occidentalis*), singleleaf ash (*Fraxinus anomala*), cliffrose (*Cowania mexicana*), and Apache plume (*Fallugia paradoxa*). Mesquite (*Prosopis glandulosa*), a thorned member of the legume family, is common in exposed stream beds. When these plants are in bloom, the stream beds and basins stand out dramatically against the surrounding desert.

HIGH PRESSURE
WATER LINE
KEEP OFF

Part of the origianl cross-canyon pipeline intersects the trail above Indian Garden.

Indian Garden Ranger Station, 4.6 miles (7.4 km) down the trail from the South Rim, is a welcome sight to weary hikers.

INDIAN GARDEN

Indian Garden has long been a focal point for human activity in Grand Canyon. Groundwater seeping through the rock layers above is stopped by the impervious Bright Angel Shale and comes out here in several springs. These springs were first used by prehistoric humans, and after AD 1300, the Havasupai Indians farmed the area seasonally. More recent use has centered around mining and finally tourism.

The Bright Angel Shale, which comprises the middle formation of the Tonto Group, was once mud on the bottom of a shallow Cambrian sea. About 510 million years ago, marine life underwent an incredible increase in diversity and density. Multicellular animals first appeared at this time. Trilobites developed and rose to a prominent position in the sea, a position they would maintain for the next 250 million years. Brachiopods, sea worms, and complex algae also appeared during this period.

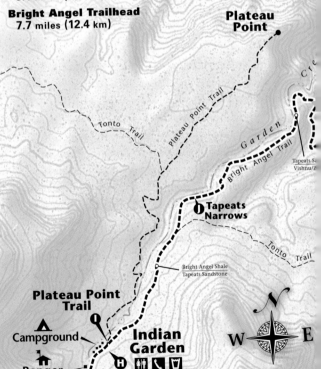

INDIAN GARDEN TO:

Bright Angel Trailhead
4.6 miles (7.4 km)

Plateau Point
1.5 miles (2.4 km)

River Trail Junction
3.1 miles (5.0 km)

Bright Angel Campground
4.7 miles (7.6 km)

Phantom Ranch
5.0 miles (8.0 km)

RIVER TRAIL JUNCTION TO:

Bright Angel Campground
1.6 miles (2.4 km)

Phantom Ranch
1.9 miles (3.1 km)

Indian Garden
3.1 miles (5.0 km)

Bright Angel Trailhead
7.7 miles (12.4 km)

Pipe Cr
Rapi

Plateau
Point

Cre

Tonto Trail

Plateau Point Trail

Garden

Bright Angel Trail

Tapeats Sa
Vishnu/2

Tapeats
Narrows

Tonto Trail

Bright Angel Shale
Tapeats Sandstone

Plateau Point
Trail

Campground

Ranger
Station

Indian
Garden

3,760 ft (1,146 m)

N
W E
S

🚻 📞 🗑
**Phantom
Ranch**
**2,546 ft
(776 m)**

**Ranger
Station**

▲
Campground

North
Kaibab
Trail

South
Kaibab
Trail

🚻 📞
**River
Resthouse
2,400 ft
(732 m)**

C O L O R A D O   R I V E R

Ⓜ **River Trail**

River Trail

**Silver
Bridge** Ⓝ

Bright Angel Rapid

Bright Angel Creek

0   0.5 Kilometer

0   0.5 Miles

Bright Angel Trail
Indian Garden to Phantom Ranch

Ⓚ **Devils
Corkscrew**

*Burro
Springs*

PLATEAU POINT TRAIL

The Plateau Point Trail heads north from Indian Garden across the Tonto Platform. This relatively flat trail is a favorite with hikers and mule riders because its terminus offers an excellent view of the Inner Gorge and the Colorado River. In the Tonto desert, only 4 inches (10 cm) of precipitation fall annually, while summer temperatures often reach 110 degrees F (43°C). The most prominent form of vegetation is blackbrush (*Coleogyne ramosissima*), while several species of cacti, banana yucca (*Yucca baccata*), and Utah agave (*Agave utahensis*) also populate the area.

Utah agave, prickly pear cactus, and blackbush along the Plateau Point Trail

A number of animal species inhabit this arid platform, including the white-tailed antelope squirrel (*Ammospermophilus leucurus*), cactus mouse (*Peromyscus eremicus*), and desert bighorn sheep (*Ovis canadensis nelsoni*).

Below the Tapeats Sandstone (which you are standing on at Plateau Point), the sequence is broken. On the north side of the canyon, however, you will notice that there are several geologic formations between the Vishnu Schist in the Inner Gorge and the Tapeats. These layers are known as the Grand Canyon Supergroup and were deposited between 740 million and 1.25 billion years ago by seas, swamps, and rivers. The brilliantly red Hakatai Shale is one of the more prominent members of this group.

The view of the Inner Gorge of the Colorado River from Plateau Point

GARDEN CREEK AND THE TAPEATS NARROWS

Directly below Indian Garden you enter a narrows through the Tapeats Sandstone. The Tapeats forms the lowermost strata in the Tonto Group and lies directly on top of the Vishnu Schist. The contact between the Tapeats and the Vishnu here is called the Great Unconformity. After the deposition of the Grand Canyon Supergroup, faults occurred, pushing the rock up and tilting it. In most places in Grand Canyon, erosion was so extensive that these rocks, over time, disappeared, leaving a 1.25-billion-year gap in time. This gap is called the Great Unconformity.

Pancaked layers of Tapeats Sandstone in the Tapeats Narrows

Just below Indian Garden a sign warns hikers, *do not attempt to hike from the rim to the river and back in one day.*

Around AD 1100, ancestral Puebloan groups inhabited the area along Garden Creek; these people built granaries and dwellings in the Tapeats cliffs. Garden Creek provided a permanent source of water for drinking and irrigation. They raised a number of crops including corn, beans, and squash, and made extensive use of the natural resources in the canyon. Banana yucca provided a food source while its fibers were used to make sandals, rope, and baskets. The ancestral Pueblo also roasted the agave plant in large pits, which can still be found throughout the canyon. Hunting comprised a major part of the ancestral Puebloan economy. Points for spears and arrows were fashioned from native materials and were used in hunting mule deer, desert bighorn sheep, squirrels, and rabbits. All of these animals are still found in Grand Canyon.

A summer hiker cools off in Garden Creek. *Do not drink untreated water from Garden or Pipe Creeks.*

A small saddle at the base of the Tapeats divides Garden Creek and Pipe Creek, the latter flowing to the Colorado River through a series of pools and chutes.

THE DEVILS CORKSCREW

The switchbacks known as the Devils Corkscrew and the long traverse through the Vishnu Schist provide a dramatic counterpoint to the lush streamside habitats above and below.

Willows and nonnative cottonwoods give way to desert vegetation. The flora in this part of the Inner Gorge adapted to growth under dry conditions. The best examples are various species of cacti, which can tolerate high temperatures, a great deal of sunlight, and very little water. Mormon tea (*Ephedra viridis*), narrowleaf yucca (*Yucca angustissima*), and mesquite are other plants that are found in the area.

COLUMBINE SPRING AND PIPE CREEK JUNCTION

Columbine Spring, which comes out of a cliff to the west of the Bright Angel Trail, forms a microhabitat in which maidenhair ferns (*Adiantum capillus-veneris*), mosses, and herbs can survive. Wildflowers, including yellow columbine (*Aquilegia chrysantha*) and scarlet monkeyflower (*Mimulus cardinalis*), can occasionally be seen during the spring and summer months. Various species of willows thrive alongside horsetails (*Equisetum* spp.) and an introduced species, tamarisk (*Tamarix chinensis*).

Many insects make the stream waters and associated riparian vegetation their homes. In turn, frogs, toads, and reptiles feed on these populations. Bird species that may be seen include American dippers (*Cinclus mexicanus*), spotted sandpipers (*Actitis macularia*), and occasionally snowy egrets (*Egretta thula*), which are transient in the region.

The Bright Angel and River Trails meet where Pipe Creek enters the Colorado River. The River Resthouse, which is located here, has an emergency telephone.

The River Resthouse, completed by the CCC in1936, features welcome shade and an emergency phone.

THE RIVER TRAIL

The Civilian Conservation Corps constructed the River Trail between 1933 and 1936 to enable hikers and mule riders to reach Phantom Ranch from the Bright Angel Trail.

Along the River Trail, the vertical walls of Vishnu Schist rise more than 1,400 feet (427 m) above you. Roughly 1.7 billion years old, the Vishnu Schist was deposited during the Precambrian period as ocean deposits mixed with volcanic ash and lava flows. Crustal slabs driven deep below the surface melted under pressure. The resulting magma squeezed into the overlying rock to form veins of red Zoroaster Granite.

The River Trail also passes through a sand dune habitat. This unstable substrata poses unique adaptational problems for the plant species that live here.

CCC workers constructing the River Trail during the 1930s

29

The Grand Canyon rattlesnake is uncommon along the Bright Angel Trail, but if you encounter a rattler, give it plenty of room.

Water drains deep into the sand shortly after it rains. Erosion and shifting of the dunes caused by wind are also a problem. Nevertheless, beavertail cactus (*Opuntia basilaris*) and prickly pear cactus (*Opuntia* spp.), sacred datura (*Datura meteloides*), and narrow-leaf yucca have managed to establish populations here. Many respond almost immediately to rain by growing root hairs through which they absorb moisture. Shortly after, they shed them to prevent evaporation. Animals, being mobile, can utilize the plant and insect food sources of the dunes while establishing homes in the more stable areas. Numerous reptiles are found here, as they are along other sections of the Bright Angel Trail. The western whiptail lizard (*Cnemidophorus tigris*) is abundant. Chuckwallas (*Sauromalus obesus*), desert collared lizards (*Crotaphytus insularis*), and the Grand Canyon rattlesnake (*Crotalus viridis abyssus*) may also be found.

THE SILVER BRIDGE

The Silver Bridge was constructed in the late 1960s to support the pipeline carrying water from Roaring Springs to the South Rim.

Boulders along the Colorado testify that the forces of erosion are slowly breaking down the rock layers above. Carried to the bottom of the canyon by water and gravity, then deposited primarily at the mouth of side tributaries, they are smoothed and rounded by moving water. Prior to the construction of Glen Canyon Dam upstream, the muddy Colorado (Spanish for "colored") carried as much as 380,000 tons (345,000 metric tons) of sediment per day past this point. This sediment load, along with seasonal flooding, periodically scoured the canyon and removed many of these boulders. Today, the river carries only about 40,000 tons (36,300 metric tons) daily, as much of the sediment is trapped behind the dam. Research scientists are studying the effects the dam has had on the Colorado River ecosystem. They know that native fishes like the Colorado River squawfish (*Ptychocheilus lucius*) and the humpback chub (*Gila cypha*), which were adapted to the pre-dam warmer, muddier water, are becoming extinct in the cold, clear water now being released from the depths of the dam.

ning the Colorado River below the mouth of Bright Angel Creek, Silver Bridge is used only by hikers. Mule trains continue along the river, crossing via the Kaibab Bridge upstream.

Hiking in Grand Canyon can be dangerous—even for experienced hikers in top physical condition. Temperatures can be extreme, water is scarce, and the terrain is often steep and unstable. The canyon environment is remote, harsh, and unforgiving. Please use the utmost caution in planning and while spending time in the canyon. You are responsible for your safety and well-being.

Copyright © 2004 by the Grand Canyon Association

Text by Scott Thybony

Alan Berkowitz wrote the original Bright Angel Trail Guide.

Scott Thybony revised and fully updated this edition.

Photography credits: Todd R. Berger for Grand Canyon Association 6–7, 13, 15, 16, 17, 18, 20, 21, 24, 24–25, 26, 27 (top), 27 (bottom), 29 (top), 30, 31; Grand Canyon National Park Museum Collection 2–3 (#18830), 5 (#10993 by Nick Berezenko), 8 (#1617 by James Eden), 9 (#7729 by Ellsworth and Emery Kolb), 28–29 (#3973E); Emery Kolb Collection, Cline Library, Northern Arizona University, Flagstaff, Arizona, and Grand Canyon National Park Museum Collection 12 (#5431 by Ellsworth and Emery Kolb).

Art Direction: Ron Short; Design: Larry Lindahl; Maps: Bronze Black

Printed on recycled paper using soy-based ink.

Cover: Bright Angel Trail below Three-Mile Resthouse. Photograph © Tom Bean

GRAND CANYON ASSOCIATION
www.grandcanyon.org

ISBN-13: 978-093821609-4

9 780938 216094

$3.95